UNDERSEA UNIVERSITY™

Underwater Exploration

by **Emily Sohn** • with **Nicole Kleinsinger** Consultant

SCHOLASTIC INC.

New York Toronto London Auckland Sydney Mexico City New Delhi Hong Kong Buenos Aires

Emily Sohn
WRITER

Emily writes about science, health, and adventure travel for both kids and adults. Though she has been scuba diving in Thailand and the Bahamas, she lives in Minneapolis, Minnesota, where she loves to explore the area's thousands of lakes by canoe. During the long winter months, she admires water in its solid form—ice and snow!

Nicole Kleinsinger
CONSULTANT

Nicole is a marine biologist, naturalist, and dive instructor. She lives in California and works with the Oceanic Society, leading natural history and research expeditions around the world.

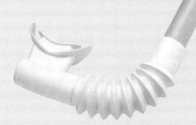

ISBN: 0-439-71186-X

Copyright © 2005 by Scholastic Inc.

Illustrators: Yancey C. Labat, Ed Shems

Photos:

Front cover: Copyright 2003 Harbor Branch Oceanographic Institution. Back cover: Jeff Hunter/Photographer's Choice/Getty Images. Title page: stephanecompoint.com.

Page 2: Photodisc Green (RF)/Getty Images. Pages 4–5: Cousteau Society/Image Bank/Getty Images. Page 6: Alexis Rosenfeld/Photo Researchers. Page 7: Stephen Frink/ The Image Bank/Getty Images. Page 8: (top) Mary Evans Picture Library; (bottom) OAR/National Undersea Research Program (NURP)/Univ. of North Carolina at Wilmington (UNCW).

Page 10: (left) CCI Archives/Photo Researchers; (right) North Wind Picture Archives. Page 11: (top) Dräger Safety AG & Co. KgaA; (bottom) Courtesy Gary Wallace-Potter/Historical Diving Society.

Page 12: Bettmann/Corbis. Page 13: (top) Creative Illusions Photography; (bottom) Alexis Rosenfeld/Photo Researchers. Page 15: Creative Illusions Photography. Page 17: NOAA/TAO project.

Page 19: (1) Phillip Colla/SeaPics.com; (2) Chris A. Crumley; (3) Paolo Curto/The Image Bank/Getty Images; (4) Royalty-Free/Corbis. Page 20: (manned submersible) OAR/NURP;

(ROV) OAR/NURP/Univ. of Connecticut; (AUV) MIT Sea Grant AUV Lab. Page 24: (top) OAR/NURP/JAMSTEC; (bottom) OAR/NURP/Univ. of Hawaii. Page 25: (Alvin) Rod Catanach/Woods Hole

Oceanographic Institution; (bathysphere) Bettmann/Corbis; (Trieste) Phil Finkle, ex-FT3, USN 1957-1961. Page 26: (top) University of New Brunswick Saint John. Pages 26 (bottom) and 27:

Rod Catanach/Woods Hole Oceanographic Institution. Page 28: Deep Sea Systems International, Inc. Page 29: Institute for Exploration, Mystic, Connecticut. Page 30: Dan Fornari/Woods Hole

Oceanographic Institution. Page 31 (top) Australian Centre for Field Robotics; (bottom) Hydroid, Inc. Page 35: (top) Mary Evans Picture Library; (bottom) Bettmann/CORBIS. Page 37:

(top) Bettmann/CORBIS; (bottom) Brian J. Skerry/National Geographic Images. Page 38: (top) OAR/NURP; (bottom) Brian J. Skerry/National Geographic Images. Pages 39 and 44:

(map) NASA/R. Stöckli/Robert Simmon/GSFC/MODIS. Page 39: (bottom) Jeffrey Howe/Visuals Unlimited. Pages 40–41: Courtesy NOAA and UNCW. Page 42: UNCW/NURP. Pages 43 (top)

and 45–46: stephanecompoint.com. Page 44: (bottom) Photo Researchers. Page 48: (top) Sai Sarkis/Photodisc/Getty Images; (bottom) UNCW/NURP.

12 11 10 9 8 7 6 5 4 3   7 8 9/0

Printed in the U.S.A.

First Scholastic printing, April 2005

The publisher has made every effort to ensure that the activities in this book are safe when done as instructed. Adults should provide guidance and supervision whenever the activity requires.

Table of Contents

page 21

Your Deep-Sea

Have you ever wondered what it's like to breathe underwater? Or pilot a submarine? Or discover sunken treasure on the seafloor? Well, ocean explorer, you're about to find out. Because in this Undersea U book, you'll discover how people dive, work, explore, and even *live* underwater for days at a time. Prepare to plunge in and explore questions like these:

- What kinds of equipment do people need to breathe underwater?

- What types of vehicles take people to the depths?

- How deep can people go?

- What kinds of work do people do underwater?

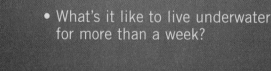

- What's it like to live underwater for more than a week?

- How do underwater robots work?

- What's it like to steer a submarine?

- How do explorers find shipwrecks and sunken cities?

Journey Begins Here!

Ready, Set, Get Wet!

As you know, ocean explorer, you live on a wet planet—oceans cover more than 70 percent of Earth's surface. The average depth of the ocean is about 12,000 feet (3,660 m), which is the same as about ten 100-story skyscrapers stacked on top of one another. That's a whole lot of water to explore!

And How Much of That Water Have People Checked Out?

Not much! Until scuba gear and submarines came along, people could only explore a few feet below the surface. Even now, scientists estimate that we have explored only about 20 percent of the underwater world!

What Could Be Down There?

Who knows! With recent advances in technology, the watery universe has opened up. Scuba diving, underwater vehicles, and even research labs on the seafloor have helped people discover new creatures, shipwrecks, and sunken cities full of treasure. There's still so much left to explore. So *water* you waiting for? Dive in!

0 feet	
63 ft.	*Aquarius* habitat (see page 39)
500 ft.	Deepest a diver has gone on one breath
650 ft.	Deepest light goes
1,000 ft.	Deepest a scuba diver has gone
6,000 ft.	1 mile
12,460 ft.	*Titanic*'s resting place
14,764 ft.	Deepest the manned sub *Alvin* has gone (see page 25)
16,400 ft.	Deepest the unmanned sub *ABE* has gone (see page 30)
35,791 ft.	Deepest a manned sub has gone (the *Trieste*—see page 25)
39,000 ft.	Challenger Deep, the deepest spot in the ocean

What's in This Month's Undersea Kit?

If reading about submarines makes you want to jump in one and cruise around right away, here's your chance to get closer to that dream. In this month's Undersea Kit, you'll find everything you need to build your own diving and rising sub! Turn to page 21 to get started!

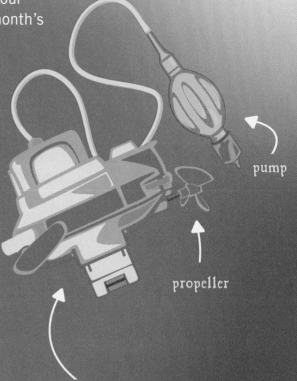

pump

propeller

Build-Your-Own Submarine Kit
Just like real submarines, your sub moves through water using a propeller.

The Undersea University Website

Looking for more deep-sea action? Then don't forget to visit **www.scholastic.com/undersea**, where you'll find a new game to continue your underwater adventures. Make sure to bring the password on the right!

WEB-SURFING PASSWORD

DEEPDOWN

PART I: Going Down, Down, Down

Okay, ocean explorer, it's time to start exploring the depths! So take a deep breath, and let's go down to the bottom of the ocean! Wait—you can't hold your breath for that long? Not to worry. People have been working on that problem for thousands of years. In this part of the book, you'll check out some of the solutions people have invented to stay under longer.

The Skinny on Skin-Diving

Before scuba gear and submarines came along, lungs were the most advanced equipment around. In ancient times, people would "skin dive" (that is, dive without any breathing equipment) in search of treasures like pearls. For each plunge, they sucked in as much air as they could before going under. To make the most of their time underwater (usually only about a minute), those early skin divers would sometimes carry stones to help them sink faster!

The First Snorkel

So, when were the first snorkels invented? Legend has it that a young Greek sailor named Scyllis first came up with the idea of breathing through a tube during the war between the Greeks and the Persians in 500 B.C.

Scyllis was captured on a Persian ship, and he dove into the sea to save his life. The Persians thought Scyllis had drowned, but little did they know! Scyllis had a clever idea—he plucked a hollow reed from the shoreline and then breathed through it while underwater to keep from being seen. He even managed to cut the Persians' ships loose (so they drifted out to sea!).

People still use snorkels today. The short tubes allow them to swim at the surface and breathe normally while checking out the view below!

When Lungs Just Aren't Enough

When it comes to diving, holding your breath will only get you so far. Pretty soon, you'll have to come up for air—no matter how much you practice. Diving bells were one of the first attempts to get around this problem.

The first diving bells were human-sized, bell-shaped containers made of metal, glass, or wood. When plunged underwater, the space inside the bell stayed filled with air, so people could hang out inside and breathe. Or, if they wanted to, divers could swim around outside the bell and then go back inside for a gulp of air.

More Oxygen, Please!

At first, a diving bell worked only as long as the oxygen inside could last—less than 20 minutes or so, depending on the bell's size. Then, in 1690, English scientist Edmund Halley figured out how to deliver fresh air into a diving bell. People on the surface would send down weighted barrels of air, and these could be attached to the bell with hoses. This invention allowed people to spend a whole hour and a half underwater, at depths of up to 66 feet (20 m).

English scientist John Smeaton developed an even better system in 1788—an air pump that delivered a constant supply of fresh air to the bell. There was even backup air in case the pump failed. That invention was like a breath of fresh air!

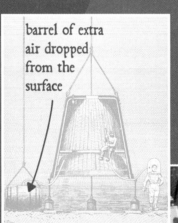

barrel of extra air dropped from the surface

Scientist Edmund Halley proposed that a diver could wear a smaller bell over his head to leave the main diving bell for short explorations.

air inside

Divers have used bells in modern times as dry places to communicate with each other and with people on land.

Saved by the Bell

Now you know how diving bells helped early divers extend their time underwater. Still, you might be wondering: How is it possible that water doesn't flood the bell? Good question! Find out the answer for yourself with this mini-bell that you can make in your own kitchen!

What You Need

- Clear pitcher or vase, or 2-liter soda bottle with the top cut off
- Water
- Crumpled-up tissue
- Small, clear drinking glass
- Tape

What You Do

I. Fill a pitcher, vase, or bottle about two-thirds full with water.

2. Tape a crumpled-up tissue to the bottom of a glass. This will be your underwater "explorer."

3. Turn the drinking glass upside down. Holding the glass level, push it down until it's completely underwater.

4. Look at the tissue in the glass. Does it look like it's still dry?

5. Remove the glass, still keeping it upside down. Dry off your fingers, then inspect the tissue. Is it wet or dry?

Sea the Point?

If you kept the glass level and upside down, the tissue inside your diving bell should have stayed completely dry. This is because a pocket of air stays trapped in the glass when you submerge it.

Why doesn't water push the air out and flood the glass? The reason is that air is lighter than water. So when a diving bell goes under, the air rises and stays trapped inside the bell, leaving no room for water to get in—and plenty of air for divers to breathe!

Bubblehead!

To spend even *more* time underwater without the burden of a big bell, people in the early 1800s started getting their air through dive helmets. This invention gave a whole new meaning to the term "airhead"!

There are three main types of dive helmets:

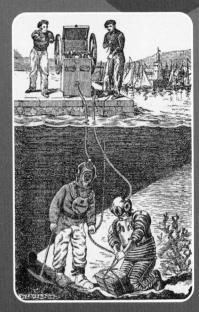

Air Helmets

In an air helmet, air is pumped into the helmet through a long hose that extends up to the surface. With this kind of helmet, divers can't go very deep, which is why they're also called "shallow water helmets." These were the earliest types of helmets.

Regulator Helmets

Invented in 1865, regulator helmets use a tank of air on the diver's back, which you can see on the left. The tank doesn't hold very much air, though, so it's attached to a hose that runs up to the surface.

The helmet is called a "regulator helmet" because there's a valve that "regulates" or controls the flow of air. When the diver breathes in, the valve lets in high-pressure air from the tank and makes it breathable by reducing its pressure. When the diver breathes out, the valve releases the air into the water.

With a regulator helmet, the diver can disconnect the air hose that comes down from the surface and explore freely, breathing from the air tank—but not for long, because the tank doesn't hold much air.

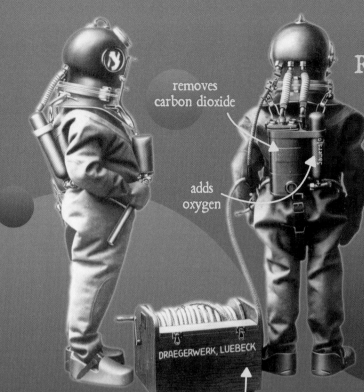

removes
carbon dioxide

adds
oxygen

rope lifts and lowers diver,
since it's hard to swim
wearing weighted shoes

DRAEGERWERK, LUEBECK

Rebreather Helmets

In a rebreather helmet, the diver can keep breathing the same air over and over again. Invented in 1911, these helmets work by removing some carbon dioxide (which people exhale) and replacing it with a little fresh oxygen from a small tank on the diver's back.

Rebreather helmets give divers more freedom than the other helmets because they don't depend on air from the surface.

Whale of a Tale

Diver to the Rescue!

Thanks to dive helmets, an ancient cathedral still stands today. The Winchester Cathedral in the United Kingdom was built in 1079 on top of a marsh, which wasn't strong enough to hold up the building. To save the sinking cathedral, diver William Walker spent six long years, from 1906 to 1912, reinforcing the structure from underwater while wearing an air helmet. His success helped make him one of the most famous dive-helmet divers (known as "hard-hat divers") in the world!

William Walker preparing for a dive

Now We're Swimming:
The Birth of Modern Scuba Diving

At first, underwater exploration was an activity available only to a small number of people who had access to clunky and expensive equipment. All that changed in the 1940s, when advances in technology made scuba diving something almost anyone could do.

Introducing...the Aqua-Lung!

You can thank the famous French marine explorer Jacques Cousteau (see the Whale of a Tale below) and his colleague Emil Gagnon for making diving available to everyone. Their 1943 invention—the Aqua-Lung—was a face mask connected by a hose to a tank of compressed air. This compact device held enough air for divers to stay underwater for hours, with nothing connecting them to the surface and without the need for a big, clunky helmet. Suddenly, diving was simple enough that any ordinary person could go diving just for fun!

INFO BUBBLE

What's in the Tank?

On land, we breathe a mixture of gases, and the same is true underwater. Scuba tanks hold combinations of nitrogen, oxygen, argon, and helium. One major difference is that the air people breathe underwater is *compressed*, or crammed in really tight. When filled with compressed air, a regular scuba tank can hold the same amount of air normally found in a phone booth!

Dive In with Jacques Cousteau!

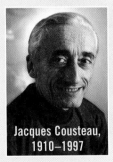

Jacques Cousteau, 1910–1997

You can't talk about underwater exploration without mentioning Jacques Cousteau. Born in France in 1910, Cousteau always loved the water as a child. Later, he became interested in machines and films, and he spent time in the French navy. All of these interests eventually merged into a career as a world-famous underwater explorer, inventor, filmmaker, and author.

In 1950, Cousteau opened new possibilities in ocean research by turning an old navy ship into a huge floating laboratory full of the most high-tech equipment around. Since then, his adventures have inspired countless numbers of people to explore, research, make films, and pursue their dreams.

Gear Up to Go Under!

Scuba stands for **S**elf-**C**ontained **U**nderwater **B**reathing **A**pparatus. Ready to take the plunge? Here's what you'll need:

Regulator and air tank: You'll carry your own tank of air and breathe through a regulator, a device that regulates the flow and lowers the pressure of the air from the tank (you can see the regulator in the diver's mouth below). When you inhale, a valve opens in the regulator and draws air from the tank. When you breathe out, the air is released into the water.

Mask: Open your eyes underwater and what do you see? Probably just a blur. Your eyes can't focus well in water, so a mask traps a pocket of air for you to look through, letting you see clearly and enjoy all the cool sights underwater!

Fins: Fins help you swim faster and more easily than you can with just your feet.

Wetsuit (or dry suit): Don't let hot weather or warm water fool you. It's easy to get cold when you go swimming. Even warm water, around 80 degrees F (27 degrees C), is much cooler than a person's normal body temperature. For insulation, you can wear a wetsuit made of a rubber-like material called *neoprene foam*. Wetsuits trap a thin layer of water inside the suit that gets heated up by your body and helps you stay warm. In extremely cold water, you can wear a "dry suit," which keeps water out completely. Underneath, you can wear long underwear or fleece pajamas!

Buoyancy control device: This inflatable vest comes with a hand-activated pump. To go down, you let air out of the vest. After you've surfaced at the end of the dive, you can fill the vest completely with air so you can float (or swim) until a dive boat picks you up.

Emergency regulator: A backup regulator can be a lifesaver if something goes wrong. Another diver can breathe through your emergency regulator, too, and share your air.

Dive watch or computer: These instruments show time, depth, and other information that helps you dive safely.

Depth and pressure gauge: Use this to keep track of your depth and air supply.

BUBBLE QUIZ

How old do you think you have to be to get your scuba certification?

A) 10   **B)** 16
C) 18   **D)** 20

Check your answer on page 48!

Going Way Down

Want to go really deep—like 1,970 feet (600 m) deep? The JIM suit, developed in 1971, is like a space suit for deep-sea divers. It allows people to move around at depths usually reserved only for underwater vehicles.

Here you can see a modern version of a JIM suit, called a Newtsuit.

"Sea" What I Mean?

What You Need

- Your sea smarts

Imagine you're scuba diving, and you have something very important to say to a fellow diver. What do you do? Don't panic! You don't have to swim to the surface or try to speak underwater somehow. You can "talk" with your hands!

Divers have lots of hand signals they can use to communicate. Many are standard around the world. Try this Sea Quest to see if you can figure out what some of them mean!

What You Do

Below you can see twelve signals that real divers use to communicate underwater. See how many of them you can figure out! Just match each hand signal on the left with its meaning on the right. When you're done, you can check your answers on page 48!

Other Ways of Communicating Underwater

Hand signals aren't the only way that divers communicate underwater. Here are three more ways:

Writing messages on a reusable board: Divers use a wipe-off surface and special pens to write underwater.

Radio helmets: Commercial and research divers wear helmets with communication equipment that uses radio waves (like walkie-talkies).

Tapping on air tanks: Sound travels very well through water, and this is a great way to get someone's attention, especially from far away. The object used to tap on the tank should be made of metal to make enough noise.

Match these words to the signals on the left:

I. Shark

2. I'm okay

3. Let's go up

4. Angelfish

5. Calm down (or slow down)

6. I'm low on air

7. Eel

8. This is cool

9. Crab

IO. Danger

II. Butterfly fish

I2. You lead, I'll follow

Sea the Point?

So, ocean explorer, how many of the signals were you able to figure out? You probably noticed that a lot of them were like pantomime (acting out a word), especially the animal signals like angelfish and crab. Divers use the animal signals to point out an animal they've seen to a fellow diver.

What's this diver saying? Check your answer on page 48!

Oh, the Pressure!

Divers have to deal with lots of pressure—but it's not the "Clean your room! Do your homework!" kind of pressure you might be used to. Pressure underwater comes from the force of all that water weighing down on the diver's body.

If you've ever been swimming in the deep end of a pool before, you know that you don't actually feel this weight on

your body. When you're underwater, you feel weightless, like you're in space! You only feel the effects of water pressure on parts of your body where there's air inside, like your inner ears (where you might feel a squeezing or pinching sensation as the air inside adjusts to the new pressure).

Water pressure gets stronger and stronger the deeper you go (because there's more and more water on top of you!). To get a good sense of how powerful the pressure can be, try this Sea Quest!

What You Need
- Large bucket
- Water
- Large plastic bag
- Drinking straw
- Quart-size jar, mostly full of water

What You Do
Part 1: Handy Diver

Water is heavy stuff—heavier than you might think. Try this activity to get a feel for it!

1. Fill a bucket with water, leaving about 5 inches (13 cm) free at the top.

2. Dip the bottom of a plastic bag into the water and drape the opening of the bag over the rim.

3. Put your hand into the bag and reach down toward the bottom of the bucket. How does your hand feel at the bottom?

Part 2: Air Slurpee

Here's another way you can feel how water pressure gets stronger the deeper you go!

1. Put one end of a straw into a jar of water, with the tip of the straw just below the surface, and blow through the straw.

2. Now, put the end of the straw near the bottom of the jar and blow again. Is it harder to blow bubbles into the top or bottom of the jar?

Sea the Point?

On land, there's a certain amount of air pushing down on us all the time. Even though you can't see it, air actually has weight! At sea level, the amount of air pressure is measured as one "atmosphere." When you go higher up—on a mountain or an airplane, for example—there's less air, which means there's less air pressure.

In water, the opposite happens. The deeper you go, the more pressure there is, because there's more and more water on top of you. And water weighs much more than air. (Try lifting that bucket of water if you want to see how heavy water can be!) Every 33 feet (10 m) of depth adds another whole atmosphere of pressure.

In Part 1, you felt the weight of water as you pushed your hand to the bottom of the bucket—it was much harder to push your hand down through the water than it would have been to push it through thin air! That's because you had to push aside the heavy water.

In Part 2, you should have found that it was harder to blow bubbles into the bottom of the jar. That's because the air you were blowing had to fight against the weight of the water. The deeper you lowered the straw, the more pressure there was on the air you were trying to blow.

Our bodies aren't used to dealing with all that pressure, so divers have to follow special procedures to help their bodies adjust. Try the next Sea Quest to find out more about the pressures of diving!

Check out what water pressure can do to a foam cup! The one on the right is the original size. The one on the left was sent down 6,600 feet (2,000 m) below the surface. Under the enormous pressure down there, the air inside the foam got squished, and the cup shrunk!

Bubble Trouble

When you dive deep underwater, ocean explorer, you might not feel any different. But the water pressure *is* causing changes to your body—particularly to the gases in your blood.

Did you know that you have gases in your blood? It's true—every time you take a breath, your lungs take in gases like oxygen and nitrogen, and the gases dissolve into your blood.

During a dive, the water pressure makes it possible for *extra* nitrogen to dissolve into your blood. Having extra gas isn't a problem on its own, but you'll encounter trouble if you come to the surface too fast. What happens? Check out this Sea Quest!

What You Do

1. Gently shake one soda bottle.

2. Over a sink, unscrew the top of the bottle. What happens?

3. Gently shake another soda bottle, then let it sit for two minutes.

4. Very slowly, unscrew the cap until you hear a hiss. Wait another minute.

5. Repeat step 4 until you can take the cap off without any hissing.

What You Need

- Two unopened bottles of soda
- A watch or timer

Sea the Point?

Your soda bottles had two things in common with scuba divers: pressure and gas!

Under high pressures, gas dissolves into liquid more easily. Carbonated drinks have carbon dioxide gas dissolved into them under high pressure (that's what makes soda fizzy). When you unscrewed the cap of the first soda bottle, there was suddenly much less pressure inside the bottle, and the dissolved gas became "undissolved," turning into lots of bubbles (and a big mess!).

Like the gas dissolved in the carbonated drink, lots of nitrogen gas can dissolve into a diver's blood under high pressure, too. If the diver comes to the surface too quickly, the water pressure around the diver drops quickly, and the gas in the diver's blood will react like the gas in the soda bottle. Bubbles of nitrogen will form in the diver's blood, causing aches, pains, and other problems. This condition is called decompression sickness, or "the bends."

To avoid decompression sickness, divers come up to the surface slowly. This allows the diver's body to get rid of the extra nitrogen by exhaling it, slowly and safely. You did the same thing when you slowly opened your second soda bottle, letting the gas out bit by bit.

Take Only Pictures, Leave Only Bubbles:
Rules for the Recreational Diver

Rules, rules, rules. Everywhere you turn, someone tells you what you can and can't do. Diving is no exception! The rules of the underwater world are designed to protect divers and the animals they encounter.

Each of the divers below is breaking an underwater rule. What is it? See if you can pick the correct rule for each one. You can check your answers on page 48.

manta ray

I
A. When grabbing a manta ray, a diver should always go for the tail, not the top.
B. This manta ray is too small for riding.
C. Divers shouldn't ride animals at all.

2
A. Divers shouldn't take anything out of the water, except if they find trash or litter.
B. Divers should wear gloves when they collect animals to avoid hurting them.
C. Divers should only collect old shells, not living animals.

3
A. Fish prefer chocolate. If you plan to feed them, make sure to bring some extra candy bars with you.
B. Don't feed or hold marine animals. It can hurt them *and* you.
C. Divers should only feed fish, not eels.

eel

coral

4
A. Coral isn't as strong as it looks! Make sure to stand on one foot only.
B. You should only stand on coral while wearing thick boots, not just fins. Otherwise you might cut your feet!
C. Touching coral can cause permanent damage to the reef. Don't do it!

PART 2: Underwater Vehicles

Swimming and diving are great ways to explore the ocean, but if you want to go *really* deep or stay under for a long time, you need a craft specially designed for underwater travel. Vehicles like this are called "submersibles," and they come in all sorts of shapes and sizes. In this part of the book, you'll learn about the different types of submersibles, how they work, and even what it's like to drive one! First, check out the main kinds of submersibles below.

Manned Submersible

Manned submersibles can take a few passengers underwater for a few hours. They're great for research and exploration, and they can also be used to work on underwater cables and oil rigs.

Remotely Operated Vehicle (ROV)

If a mission is supposed to go really deep, it's often more practical to send down a robot instead of people. Wires connect an ROV to a ship on the surface, where a pilot uses a remote control to tell the ROV to take pictures, collect samples, and send back data.

Automatic Underwater Vehicle (AUV)

AUVs are like ROVs, but without the wires. Loaded with instruments, these robots work pretty much on their own to collect lots of different kinds of data and samples quickly and efficiently. Some can stay underwater for months!

To learn more about how submersibles work, check out the next page----the Sea Quest shows you how to make your own!

Make Your Own Submarine!

What You Need
- Build-Your-Own Submarine Kit
- Bathtub or bucket of water

What's the best way to plunge into the world of submarines? Try making your own! With your Build-Your-Own Submarine Kit, you'll be able to construct a sub that rises and sinks by adding and releasing air, just like a real sub. So roll up your sleeves, ocean explorer. It's time to get to work!

What You Do
Part 1: Putting It All Together

1. To get started, turn the bottom half of the sub upside down and insert the two weight holders into the slots so they face each other. Then slide the weights into the holders.

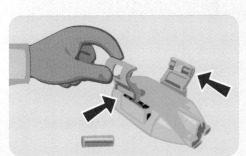

2. Turn the bottom half of the sub right side up, standing it up on the weights. Slide the long metal rod through the hole in the back of the sub, making sure the white gear rests in place at the front, as shown. Then push the propeller onto the end of the rod.

3. Drop the round, hollow gear piece through the hole in the bottom of the sub.

4. Place the gear with the hook attached to it into the slot in front of the gear you just added, as shown.

5. Now place the smallest gear in the slot in front of the hooked gear. When you turn this gear, it should make the propeller spin. (Test it out!)

21

6. Place the remaining gear in the slot next to the hooked gear, with the plain side facing the front of the sub. Now, when you turn the hook, all of the gears should turn, too.

7. Loop all three rubber bands around the hook, then attach them to the hook on the back of the sub.

8. Place the rod with the flat tabs at each end across the front of the sub.

9. Snap the plastic cover into place over the gears—all the wind-up parts are now set up! Turn the crank on the bottom to test them—the propeller should spin when you let go.

10. Now, attach the top half of your sub. First, hook the front ends of each half together. Then, snap the two pieces together at the back. (If you ever want to take your sub apart again, just press your finger into the slot at the back.)

11. Now all that's left is to attach your air pump! Slide one end of the yellow tube onto the hollow point on top of the sub, pressing it on firmly. Then attach the other end of the tube to the hollow point on the end of the pump. Your sub is now complete!

Part 2: Dive In!

Now that you've built your sub, it's time to take it for a test dive! You'll make your sub sink, rise, and move through the water, just like a real sub!

1. Fill up a tub or bucket with water and place your sub on the surface.

2. To make your sub dive, press the button on the end of the pump. This lets the air out of your sub, so it'll fill with water and sink.

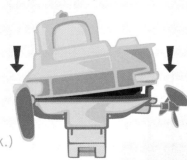

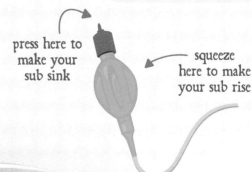

press here to make your sub sink

squeeze here to make your sub rise

3. To make your sub rise, fill it with air by squeezing the pump. The sub should float to the surface.

4. To keep your sub on the surface, pull out the button on the end of the pump (so air doesn't seep out).

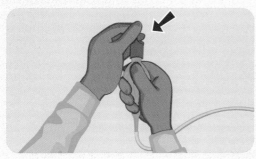

5. To make your sub move forward, wind up the propeller by turning the crank on the bottom (it will help to turn the sub upside down when you do this). Hold onto the propeller until the sub is back in the water so it doesn't start too soon.

As the propeller drives your sub through the water, you can press the button on the end of the pump to make your sub sink, then try pumping the sub full of air to make it rise as it moves!

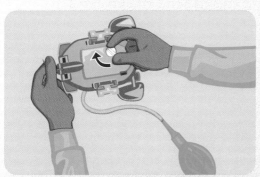

Sea the Point?

When you pushed the button on your pump to let the air out of your sub, your sub filled with water and sank. When you pumped your sub full of air, the air pushed the water back out, and your sub floated back to the surface.

Real subs work the same way! They have an inner and outer hull (or frame), and the space in between is called the *ballast tank*. The ballast tank is filled with either air or water to make the sub float or sink. When a sub needs to dive deeper, it lets in more water to make itself heavier. When it needs to get back up to the surface or just go a little higher, it fills the tank with more air, pushing out the water and making the sub lighter.

Where does that extra air come from? It's carried on the submarine in tanks of compressed air. Since the compressed air is crammed into a small space, it doesn't affect the sub's ability to sink. But when the air is released into the ballast tank, it expands to fill a larger portion of the sub, making the sub rise!

When it comes to moving *forward*, real subs move using propellers just like yours—although the motors that make real propellers turn are much more complex than your wind-up motor.

Now that you've gotten an inside look at your own sub, turn the page to learn about real submersibles that work the same way!

A Deep-Sea Ride:
Manned Submersibles

The sub you just built can't hold *people*—but real manned submersibles can. These small submarines are the best way for humans to go deep underwater. How deep? A Japanese model called the *Shinkai 6500* can reach depths of 4 miles (6.5 km)!

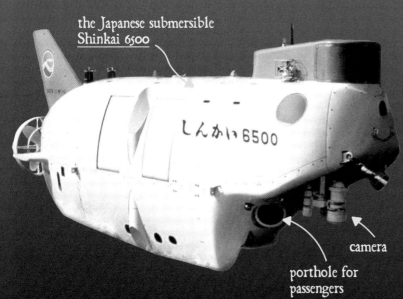

the Japanese submersible
Shinkai 6500

しんかい6500

camera

porthole for
passengers

To stand up to the serious water pressure at those depths, manned submersibles are made of tough steel. To keep the people inside safe and comfortable, the submersibles are filled with air that's at the same pressure as air on the surface.

Not Just Cool—They're Also a Useful Tool

Manned submersibles are perfect for exploring shipwrecks, like the famous *Titanic* wreck. With a submersible, pilots can navigate around obstacles and map the area. This makes further exploration with unmanned submersibles cheaper, easier, and safer. Manned submersibles are also useful for inspecting underwater structures, like communication cables, oil platforms, and bridge supports. And these little subs can go deeper than larger submarines, because their small size means they hold up better under lots of pressure.

The *Deep Rover* can take one
person 980 feet (300 m) deep.

All Aboard <u>Alvin</u>!

A cartoon chipmunk named Alvin inspired the name for the first manned deep-sea research submersible. *Alvin* made its first dive in 1964, when it went down just 35 feet (10.5 m). More than 4,000 dives later, *Alvin* can now go 14,764 feet (4,500 m) below the ocean's surface. *Alvin* runs on batteries that allow it to stay underwater for up to ten hours.

In 1979, scientists used *Alvin* to discover hydrothermal vents—bubbling plumes of hot water seeping up from the ocean floor. What was it like to be one of the first humans to lay eyes on these vents? Find out on the next page!

In 1986, *Alvin* made twelve trips to the sunken *Titanic* to photograph the wreck.

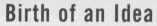

side view of <u>Alvin</u>

Birth of an Idea

Today, manned submersibles are a great way to explore new territory, but the very first ones weren't so easy to maneuver—if the passengers had any control over their direction at all! Check out two of them below.

Bathysphere: The name means "deep sphere," and that's a perfect description of the hollow steel ball that dove to 3,028 feet (923 m) in 1934. Its inventor sat inside, and a steel cable connected the bathysphere to a ship above. The bathysphere sank, then rose—there was no way to move or steer it.

Bathyscaphe: With battery-powered electric motors, bathyscaphes (BATH-ih-skafs) could dive without any connection to the surface. In 1960, the bathyscaphe *Trieste* took two people all the way down to the bottom of the Challenger Deep, the deepest part of the ocean floor, more than 35,000 feet (10,670 m) deep! No manned submersible has gone as deep since.

SUBMERSIBLE PILOT
BLee Williams

BLee Williams now works as a science technician at the University of New Brunswick, St. John, in Canada. He got his unusual nickname, short for "Bobby Lee," when he was in the navy, so he wouldn't be confused with all the other Bobs, Lees, and Williams on his submarine.

What's it like to drive a sub? Meet **BLee Williams**, a pilot who drove the submersible *Alvin* for eleven years—and more than 300 dives! Read on to meet the man behind the missions!

Question: Where did your interest in ocean exploration come from?

Answer: In my family history, I have steamship captains, lighthouse keepers, commercial fishermen, marines, and that's pretty much it. My family has lived off the sea for the last several hundred years, so it was a natural choice for me.

Q: What's it like inside *Alvin*?

A: *Alvin* consists of a sphere 6 feet (1.8 m) wide that's chock full of electronic equipment. The pilot is crouched—you sink down on your knees, and then bring your rear end onto your heels. Then you lean forward and support your weight on your forehead as you look out

Williams sitting on *Alvin* just before a dive

the front window. You're compressed like that for nine hours!

Q: What kind of science does *Alvin* do?

A: I've worked on all sorts of projects. We collect rocks for geologists; we take water samples and gather rocks for chemists; we gather live animals and dead animals for biologists; and we do a little bit of exploration work that requires mapping. All kinds of stuff like that. It's fascinating!

Q: What were some of the best parts about piloting *Alvin*?

A: Getting to work with scientists! Most of the people I took to the bottom of the ocean for their first time ever were just awed by it. They couldn't even talk. They were on sensory overload. All of a sudden it wasn't a picture anymore, not a video anymore, not a rock on somebody's shelf. It was right there in front of them, right out the window. It just can't be explained.

Q: What's the best way to prepare to be a submersible pilot?

A: We do a tremendous amount of maintenance between dives. We add and remove equipment for every dive to adapt *Alvin* to new missions. So, it's important to be good with mechanical and electrical things. You definitely have to be a good troubleshooter and problem solver!

Q: What was your favorite dive?

A: My favorite dive was on the Galapagos Ridge. This was a dive for exploration, not just to collect samples.

When we left the "known area" and drove along the ridge, we were seeing an area no human had ever seen! Scientists back on the surface were calling us on the underwater telephone, saying, "We don't think you should do what you're doing. We think you should go back, or turn left." But their information was a few minutes old, and we could see interesting things out the window. We finally told them, "We're going to do what we set out to do."

Sure enough, we stuck with our dive plan, and we discovered something really exciting!

Q: What did you discover?

A: We found evidence of animal life that had never been seen on the Galapagos Ridge before. Then, we found evidence of vents in the ocean floor where boiling-hot water had once come pouring out—only vents that released cooler water had been seen before. I didn't even finish my college education, and there I was making new discoveries like a Nobel Prize–winning scientist—and having a tremendous amount of fun!

Alvin underwater

Keep Your Head Above

So, you're all set to get in a submersible and take the plunge, right? Not so fast. In some conditions, it's just not a good idea to send people underwater. If the water's really cloudy or the currents are strong, a submersible pilot might not be able to see well enough to steer.

Likewise, some missions are too risky for people—like inspecting pipelines that could explode, or exploring new areas where there could be hidden dangers.

That's when it's time to use an unmanned vehicle, called an **ROV** (**R**emotely **O**perated **V**ehicle). If something happens to an **ROV**, no lives will be lost. These machines can also stay down a lot longer than people can—it helps that they don't have people inside who need to breathe! An **ROV** can also rescue submarines that have gotten stuck or run out of power.

The *Global Explorer*'s first mission took it to the bottom of the Arctic Ocean. Scientists on land watched a video from its cameras as they steered it over the seafloor.

Water with ROVs

Deep-Diving Robots

ROVs are basically remote-controlled robots. They range in size from just a few feet across to more than 15 feet (5 m) long. Electric cables connect an ROV to a ship at the surface, and a trained expert on the ship controls the robot's actions.

Depending on what they're designed to do, ROVs can carry a variety of equipment that allow them to "see" and "feel" like a diver would.

The Hero Hercules

Hercules is an ROV used especially for collecting artifacts from ancient shipwrecks. It's got brushes to clear off artifacts and a pair of robotic arms that can pick up small objects or push heavy ones out of the way. An operator on the surface controls the arms and tells *Hercules* what to do.

Hercules is built to withstand high pressure—it can descend up to 2.5 miles (4,000 m) below the surface.

So, what happens if a researcher has to collect a whole lot of data and doesn't have time to sit at the controls of a submersible the whole time, directing its every motion? Then it's time to try out an AUV! Turn the page to read all about

AUVs: Robots

ROVs are pretty cool, but those connector cables can be a drag—literally. **AUV**s (**A**utomatic **U**nderwater **V**ehicles) solve that problem by ditching the wires and swimming solo. These cutting-edge robots navigate all by themselves, with no direction from humans, using *sonar* technology (which uses sound waves to determine where obstacles are).

AUVs can move more quickly than ROVs, and they can work around the clock without having to wait for signals from a person on the surface. Some AUVs can stay underwater for *months* at a time!

What Can AUVs Do?

The sky (or rather, the ocean floor) is the limit! One of the best things about AUVs is that they can do lots of tasks at once. Using sonar, an AUV can count fish in a certain area. At the same time, it can use other equipment to collect information about water quality, temperature, plant life, and how rough the water is. With so much data flowing in, scientists can start solving the sea's trickiest puzzles!

The Future Is Here: A Robot Named ABE

ABE stands for **A**utomatic **B**enthic **E**xplorer. Built in the mid-1990s by scientists at the Woods Hole Oceanographic Institution in Massachusetts, *ABE* was the first underwater robot of its kind. It can dive down as low as 16,400 feet (5,000 m) and can monitor large areas over long stretches of time. Before *ABE* goes for a dive, scientists supply it with a computer program that tells it what to do while underwater. Then, all by itself, *ABE* can take pictures, make maps, record data, collect samples, and more!

Air-filled top pods keep ABE upright in water.

NCC 1701/B

ABE
WHOI • NSF

Swimming Solo!

Oh, Oberon!

Oberon, an AUV being developed in Australia, is a great ocean explorer because it's small and maneuverable—and smart! All by itself, this 5-foot (1.5-m) robot will be able to explore a coral reef, getting into tight places to take color photographs to send to scientists back on land. At the same time, it will create a map of the area.

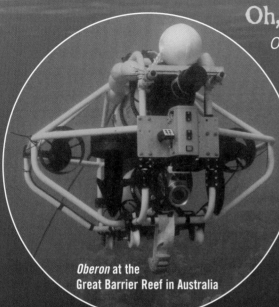

Oberon at the
Great Barrier Reef in Australia

Scientists' New Best Friend

REMUS is a small AUV with a lot of power. Just over 4 feet (1.3 m) long, *REMUS* can be equipped to record temperature, map the ocean floor, monitor the water quality, take photos and video recordings, and more!

Because *REMUS* is so compact, it's easy for scientists to use—two people in a small boat can get this AUV in and out of the water, with no need for heavy equipment to haul it up onto dry land.

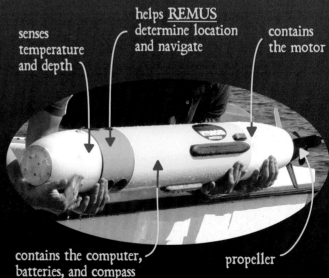

senses temperature and depth

helps **REMUS** determine location and navigate

contains the motor

contains the computer, batteries, and compass

propeller

Okay, ocean explorer, now you've had a look at all sorts of equipment for underwater exploration. Think you know your stuff? Then get ready to lead a few underwater missions of your own on the next page!

Pick Your Machine!

What You Need
- Your sub smarts

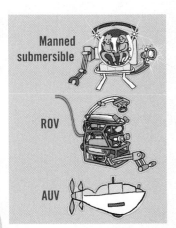

Manned submersible

ROV

AUV

Imagine you're a marine scientist preparing to do some undersea research. What kind of underwater vehicle will you use? It all depends on the nature and purpose of your expedition. See if you can pick just the right vehicle for each of the five missions in this Sea Quest!

What You Do

Read through pages 24–31 to get a sense of the strengths and weaknesses of each type of underwater vehicle. Then, tackle the scenarios below. For each one, take your pick: **Manned submersible**, **ROV**, or **AUV**? Choose wisely—your future as an ocean explorer is on the line!

1. Mystery Disaster

You need to go down 10,000 feet (3,050 m) to investigate a shipwreck. You're not the first person to visit the wreck, but you've been hired to use video and still photography to create a detailed map.

2. Hot Fish!

It's Too Hot!

I'm Moving!

ALASKA

The water off the coast of California is warmer than normal this year. It's your job to figure out how the change in water temperature is affecting fish populations. Every day for two months, you'll want to count the number of fish in an area. You'll also need to record information about the ocean, including water temperature and visibility.

3. Cure for Cancer

You're a medical researcher with big goals: You want to find a cure for cancer! There's evidence that a certain type of sponge has substances in it that fight cancer. You want to find that sponge and learn more about those substances. You know where the sponge species has turned up before. Your plan is to go back with cameras to scan the area and collect some sponges to examine back in your lab.

4. The Deepest Deep

This expedition will be extreme! You want to investigate the deepest spot in the ocean, the Challenger Deep in the Mariana Trench. The site is nearly 7 miles (11 km) below the surface, and it has never been explored before.

5. Mountain Diving

This time, you're going to study a remote, unexplored mountain range. And no, we're not talking about the Himalayas or the Alps. These mountains lie 5,000 feet (1,524 m) below the surface of the ocean! Underwater mountains, or seamounts, are home to lots of rare species. It's your job to figure out what's living down there!

Sea the Point?

How'd you do? Check your answers:

1. An **ROV** is the best choice for this situation. The wreck has already been studied before, so you don't need a manned submersible. An AUV is also not the best choice, because you'll want to be in control of what kind of data you collect. An ROV can collect the videos and photos you need as you control it from the surface!

2. In this case, an **AUV** is the best choice. You can just program in the measurements you need, then let the AUV do its thing. Because it has to take the same readings every day, using an ROV or manned submersible would be expensive and time-consuming.

3. To collect the sponges, you'll want to use an **ROV**. You've been to the area before, so you don't need to go down there yourself. And an ROV is better than an AUV here, because you'll want to direct the machine once it gets down there. ROVs also have great cameras and equipment for collecting samples.

4. You'll want to go under in a **manned submersible** for this one. The Challenger Deep is an unexplored place, and you'll need a small group of experts to interpret what you see.

5. Again, you'll want to use a **manned submersible**. Mountain ranges present plenty of obstacles that require careful navigation, and no human has ever seen this area before.

The Biggest of 'Em All:

When it comes to underwater vehicles, military submarines are about as big as they get. They're like the jumbo jets of the ocean world! Subs can be up to 660 feet (200 m) long—that's about three times the length of a big airplane! One sub can carry more than 150 people and stay down for months at a time.

Powered Up!

How does a submarine have the power to keep running for *months*? Some submarines run on a type of fuel called diesel (the same stuff big trucks use). Since diesel engines need oxygen to work, they can only run when the sub is at the surface (or just under it, with a snorkel reaching to the surface for air). The diesel engines charge up batteries that provide power when the sub is underwater.

Other subs run on nuclear power instead. Nuclear generators don't need oxygen, so the sub can stay underwater for much longer, running off engines instead of batteries. And since nuclear fuel lasts for years, the sub doesn't need to refuel for a long time.

Super Stealthy

Since military subs sometimes have to stay hidden (especially during wartime), they often have a really special feature that helps them avoid detection— a special coating on their outer surfaces that absorbs sound. That way, they can avoid being detected by sonar, a technology that locates objects underwater using sound waves. So, even the biggest sub can be practically invisible!

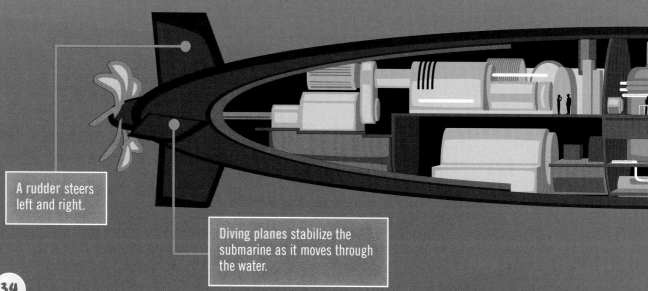

A rudder steers left and right.

Diving planes stabilize the submarine as it moves through the water.

Submarines

The hull is the body of the submarine. A typical hull is made of very strong steel. The metal can be up to 2 inches (5 cm) thick!

A radio and antenna let the crew communicate with people on the surface and on other subs. They also allow people on the surface to track the sub's exact location.

A periscope allows the crew to scan the surface from shallow depths.

Submarines: A Powerful Wartime Weapon

For a long time, submarines have been a major force in battle. Here are some early examples.

1776: The *Turtle*

American David Bushnell invented the first submarine specifically for attack. Because it looked like a sea turtle floating upright, he called it the *Turtle*. When it was time to attack, a ship hauled the *Turtle* close to its target. Its pilot  then used a foot pump to let water in and out, which made the sub sink and rise. The pilot could then use propellers to steer and a drill to put gunpowder in the hull of enemy ships. During the Revolutionary War, the United States used the *Turtle* to attack a British ship. The attack was unsuccessful, but the idea of using subs for warfare definitely caught on!

1955: The First Nuclear-Powered Sub, the *Nautilus*

 In 1955, the United States launched the first nuclear-powered submarine, the USS *Nautilus*. Over the next few years, the *Nautilus* broke all speed and distance records. In 1958, the sub went on a secret mission to become the first ship to cross the North Pole. It had to travel beneath the ice for thousands of miles to get there!

Ballast controls buoyancy, or how well the sub floats. Tanks are filled with water or air to lower or raise the sub.

Say It Like a Submariner!

Now that you're becoming an expert on submarines, you'll probably want to *sound* like an expert, too. Every field of work has its own language, and submarine work is no exception.

Here's an example to get you started: Submariners always say "shut the door," not "close the door," because "close" sounds sort of like "blow," which means "fill the tanks with air." A simple request for privacy could cause the ship to rise to the surface! That's why it's important to know your sub lingo, and this Sea Quest will give you a quick intro!

What You Need

- Your word wits

I'M GONNA DANCE WITH THE FAT LADY.

WHAT?

What You Do

Below you'll find a list of words and phrases you're likely to hear on a submarine. Can you match the lingo on the left with its meaning on the right? You can check your answers on page 48!

Submariner LINGO

1 Op
2 Officer of the Deck
3 Landlubber
4 Nonqual
5 Rig for black
6 Rig for white
7 Watch
8 People tank
9 Rack
10 Dancing with the fat lady

Meanings

A Someone who is not a sailor

B Looking through the periscope

C A submarine's operation, or mission (tracking other subs is one example)

D A six-hour work shift, which involves standing at a specific station to help run the sub

E Turn off the lights

F Someone who's not qualified to be onboard a submarine due to lack of training

G The person who commands the sub's motion, navigation, and weapons

H Bed or bunk

I Turn on the lights

J The hull, or body, of the sub

PART 3: Living with the Fish

If simply *traveling* underwater isn't exciting enough for you, you might want to try *living* down there for a while! Places underwater where people live and work are called "habitats." Read on to get the inside scoop on living with the fish!

The First on the Undersea Frontier

Jacques Cousteau (see page 12) set up the first underwater habitat, called *ConShelf One*, in 1962. Two men lived in it for seven days at a depth of 33 feet (10 m) off the coast of France. The men spent five hours a day diving. Then they returned to *ConShelf One* for food, warmth, and sleep.

Jacques Cousteau presenting his idea for an underwater habitat

What's the Point of an Underwater Habitat?

Why not just dive or take a submersible? Good question! It's all about time—with either scuba gear or a submersible craft, you'll eventually run out of air or power. Underwater habitats, on the other hand, have an unlimited supply of air and power (from hoses and cables that run up to a station on the surface). They're like hotels at the bottom of the sea! Staying down there for a while is a great way to collect data and learn more about the underwater world.

On the right is *Aquarius*, a modern habitat. Find out more about it on pages 39–41!

Hanging Out in Hydrolab

Hydrolab was one of the most famous underwater research stations of all time. Built by the National Oceanic and Atmospheric Administration, it sat on the ocean floor from 1966 to 1982. During that time, more than 700 people visited the lab. To see *Hydrolab* today, you don't even need to go near water. It's on display at the Smithsonian Institution's National Museum of Natural History in Washington, D.C.

Who Lives in Underwater Habitats?

The people who live in underwater habitats are called "aquanauts." Like astronauts, they get to spend lots of time in places that most people never go—except they visit "ocean space" instead of outer space!

Research is the biggest reason aquanauts choose to leave fresh air behind for more than a week at a time. Projects include:

- Studying animals and their habitats
- Measuring the effects of pollution on coral reefs
- Analyzing the changing nutrients in the water

From "Under" Space to Outer Space

Astronauts also use underwater habitats to train for conditions in outer space. Because people feel almost "weightless" in water, the ocean is a great substitute for space, and astronauts often practice their space-walking skills underwater before their space missions. Researchers also study how people's bodies react to living underwater to get a better idea of how weightlessness will affect people's bodies in orbit.

Aquanauts often spend more than a week at a time deep below the ocean's surface.

Welcome to Aquarius!

Okay, ocean explorer, want to get a peek inside a real undersea habitat? Then get ready to experience *Aquarius*! This underwater research lab is in the Florida Keys National Marine Sanctuary, just off the coast of Florida. It's the latest and currently the *only* undersea habitat used for research!

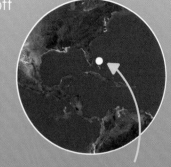

At 63 feet (19 m) deep, *Aquarius* sits next to a coral reef. Scientists usually visit the habitat for ten-day missions. Inside, they can work on computers and lab equipment like the kind they have in their labs up on the surface, and they can bring down extra equipment and belongings inside water-tight containers. And here's the cool part—they *also* spend up to nine hours each day outside in the water, scuba diving along the reef to do their research!

Aquarius, run by the University of North Carolina at Wilmington as part of NOAA's National Undersea Research Program, is located just off the Florida Keys.

Dive In, the Pressure's Fine!

Inside *Aquarius*, the air pressure is equal to the water pressure on the outside. That means you can go out for a dive and come back inside to eat, work, and sleep, without having to worry about the effects of changing pressure on your body (see page 18). When you're ready to leave *Aquarius*, you'll spend seventeen hours "decompressing" (or letting your body slowly get used to lower pressure) before you return to the surface.

So, ocean explorer, are you ready to dive in and take the grand tour of *Aquarius*? Then turn the page!

Aquarius, shown here just before it was sent down to the ocean floor, is about the size of a small school bus.

Take the Grand Tour!

To visit *Aquarius*, ocean explorer, you'll have to suit up in your scuba gear and dive down 63 feet (19 m). Then you'll swim inside the main entrance, called the wet porch. It's open to the ocean, but air pressure keeps the water out. This works sort of like an air pocket in an upside-down glass or diving bell. (Turn back to the Sea Quest on page 9 for more on this.) What's waiting for you once you step into the wet porch? Check out the inside view below!

Space? Not Much!
Aquarius is about as big as a half-sized school bus. And you'll share this little space with five other people!

Sleep Tight!
You'll sleep in a bunk bed, which are stacked three high.

Check Out the View!
Every morning, you'll wake up to a spectacular view of the ocean through a large porthole. You might just feel like you're living in an aquarium!

Got the Munchies?
Aquarius has a full kitchen, called the galley, equipped with a refrigerator and microwave oven. You'll sit around a table near the porthole and peek out at fish (and diving aquanauts!).

Plenty of Work to Do!
Workstations have computers and other lab equipment for research.

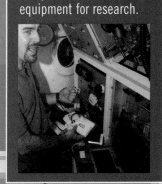

Life-Support Buoy

The Life-Support Buoy is a really important part of *Aquarius*. The buoy is a platform that floats on the surface and houses the air and power supply for *Aquarius*. The air and power are sent down to the habitat through hoses and cables.

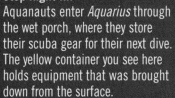

When Nature Calls...
The lab has a toilet, sink, and shower.

Step Right In!
Aquanauts enter *Aquarius* through the wet porch, where they store their scuba gear for their next dive. The yellow container you see here holds equipment that was brought down from the surface.

AQUANAUT
Leanne Rutten

Leanne Rutten knows what it's like to live and work underwater—she's been on many research missions to the undersea habitat *Aquarius*. In fact, she even had her wedding down there!

Leanne Rutten grew up in Florida with the ocean as her backyard. In school, she studied physics and biology. Now, she's a coral reef researcher at the University of North Carolina in Wilmington's National Underwater Research Center. Read on to find out what it's like to be an aquanaut!

Rutten and a fellow aquanaut inside *Aquarius*

Question: Why did you decide to become an aquanaut?

Answer: There was an unexpected immediate opening for an aquanaut, and my supervisor suggested I fill the spot. At first I was a bit nervous, but my overwhelming curiosity won. It was one of the best decisions of my life!

Q: What do you pack for an *Aquarius* mission?

A: For the type of coral reef research I usually participate in, we pack laminated site maps (which can be used in the water), compasses, cameras, measuring tapes, and all sorts of other equipment for working underwater. We dress warmly, since it does get cold down there. And I always pack a book, photos of my family, and a stash of chocolate.

Q: What's it like living underwater?

A: Living underwater is wonderful. Each hour from dawn to dusk and beyond brings constantly changing sights and sounds. Daily dive excursions reveal new discoveries—and new heartbreaks. Discarded fishing lines, old lobster traps, beer bottles, and injured fish stand out underwater. Seeing these things on a daily basis makes me realize how important it is to reduce the impacts of human activities on the oceans as much as possible.

Q: What are the biggest challenges underwater?

A: Although aquanauts are usually too excited, busy, and exhausted to become homesick, I really do miss my family while living in *Aquarius*. After a week or so, I also find myself wanting to feel a fresh breeze and warm sunshine on my face. I also miss a few junk food items that are hard to come by in *Aquarius*: ice cream (not melted), pizza (not cold), and soda (not flat).

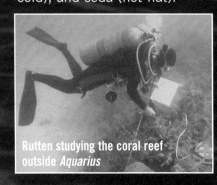

Rutten studying the coral reef outside *Aquarius*

PART 4:
Mysteries of the Deep

Underwater exploration is not just about studying the ocean and all the creatures that live in it—it's also about discovering the past. How so? Well, for starters, there are...

Shipwrecks!

For as long as ships have sailed the seas, there have been shipwrecks. When a ship goes under, it brings with it whatever was onboard—including jewelry, pottery, clothes, barrels of food, and other clues about what life was like at the time. It's like an undersea time capsule! Underwater archaeologists can get tons of great insights into the past by carefully studying these wrecks, as you'll discover in other Undersea U books.

Ships aren't the only thing preserved underwater for archaeologists to study. There are also...

Sunken Cities!

The idea of a whole city sinking beneath the sea might seem really strange, but it can happen! Earthquakes or other disasters have caused cities (or parts of cities) to sink or get covered by water. Sunken cities can remain buried under the sand for centuries before archaeologists discover them. That's when the work—and excitement—of excavation begins!

The next few pages will give you a taste of how exciting it can be to dig up a sunken city. Get your dive gear on. We're going under!

An archaeologist cleans inscriptions on an ancient stone found in the sunken city of Alexandria (turn the page for more!)

Ancient Egypt — Under the Sea

Would you believe that entire cities and magnificent monuments could sink into the sea and then lie buried for hundreds, even *thousands* of years before anyone discovers them? It's true!

Some 700 years ago, parts of the city of Alexandria (in Egypt, at the mouth of the Nile River) crumbled into the Mediterranean Sea after an earthquake. It wasn't until the twentieth century that underwater archaeologists finally started to recover some of the massive sculptures and buildings that spent centuries under the sand!

The Pharos lighthouse in ancient Alexandria

The City

Alexandria was like the New York City of the ancient world. It was beside a river and the sea, so it became a major port and the capital of Egypt soon after it was built in 332 B.C.

Without a doubt, the city was beautiful: It had all sorts of huge monuments and sculptures. And just off the coast lay an island called Pharos, with a lighthouse of the same name. At more than 400 feet (122 m) tall, the lighthouse was named one of the Seven Wonders of the World. Not only was its height and technology impressive, but it withstood more than twenty earthquakes between the fourth and fourteenth centuries A.D.!

The Sinking

Earthquakes finally got the best of Pharos and much of Alexandria in the 1300s. As the earth shook again and again, huge statues of gods and goddesses tumbled into the sea, along with buildings that lay too close to shore. The lighthouse, too, turned from an ancient wonder into a wet pile of rubble.

The Search

Divers rediscovered statues and other wreckage in the 1960s, and some mapping and salvaging followed. But it wasn't until 1994 that the Egyptian authorities allowed a major recovery effort. First, a team of French archaeologists made detailed maps of objects in the area. Then, a team of divers used salvage balloons (see page 47) to start bringing things up.

French marine archaeologist Jean-Yves Empereur, who led recovery efforts in 1994, looks at the inscriptions on this stone sphinx.

The Find

The results were spectacular! It took lots of work over several years, but the team dragged up enormous stone statue heads, structural columns, and twenty-six sphinxes (sculptures of winged monsters that have a woman's head and lion's body), among other artifacts. In all, more than 2,500 pieces were brought to the surface.

Less than 1 percent of the objects actually came from the famous Pharos lighthouse—most belonged to other monuments in Alexandria. But the pieces that *did* come from the lighthouse gave the archaeologists a good idea of what the tower looked like.

An archaeologist cleans a statue after it spent 2,000 years underwater.

The Future

There's still so much more to learn about Alexandria. What were the lives of its residents like? What was it like to look out at the Mediterranean from the top of the lighthouse? And how did the people of Alexandria build such an impressive structure?

Many artifacts still lie on the seafloor waiting to be excavated. Some will remain there forever for scuba divers to see (like an underwater museum!). Others will be brought to the surface for further study. Who knows, ocean explorer—if a career in underwater archaeology appeals to you, maybe you could join in the discovery!

Divers raise heavy objects like this stone statue base using salvage balloons. Try the Sea Quest on the next page to see how this works!

After an artifact is raised by a salvage balloon, it's hoisted out of the water by a ship. Here you can see a stone sphinx being lifted from the sea with modern Alexandria in the background.

Treasure Hunt!

It's not easy to find sunken cities and piles of treasure at the bottom of the ocean, but it sure is exciting when it happens. One of the biggest challenges is dragging all that stuff back up to the surface (called *salvaging*). Many artifacts are too heavy to lift, and bringing up little pieces one by one would take forever. Since cranes can't go underwater, marine archaeologists use balloons to salvage instead. Try this Sea Quest to see how!

sunken "treasure"

What You Need

- Bucket, basin, or bathtub with at least 6 inches (15 cm) of water
- Metal spoon
- Penny
- Metal key
- Two paper clips
- Balloon

What You Do

1. Toss a spoon, penny, key, and one paper clip into the water.

2. Blow up a balloon until it's about the size of an orange, tie it closed, and attach a paper clip to the end.

3. Push the balloon underwater and attach the paper clip on the balloon to the paper clip that's underwater.

4. Let go of the balloon and watch the salvaging!

5. Repeat steps 3 and 4 with each of the other objects, attaching the paper clip on the balloon to the object on the bottom of your tub or bucket. How much can your balloon lift? How do you think you could make it lift even more?

Sea the Point?

Air is lighter than water, so a balloon filled with air will rise to the surface, lifting objects along with it, as you should have discovered.

To do this in real life, the divers bring compressed air in tanks down to the seafloor, and they attach extra-large balloons called "salvage balloons" to the objects they want to lift—statues, stone pillars, you name it! Then, they use the compressed air to fill the balloons, causing the balloons to rise (just like your model sub rises when you fill it with air). The bigger the balloons get, the more they can lift.

You might have found that your spoon was too heavy for your balloon to lift. If so, try again with a bigger balloon! The more air you have, the more weight your balloon can lift.

Back to the Surface.... For Now!

Congratulations! You've just returned from an amazing journey through the world of ocean exploration! You learned all about scuba diving, saw all sorts of underwater vehicles, got an inside look at life in an undersea research station, and more!

There are so many ways to explore the underwater world, and there are still so many shipwrecks to discover, species to name, and mysteries to solve. So, keep your mind open to what might lie under the depths, and start preparing for your next undersea adventure now! Who knows what discoveries await you?

THE ANSWER KEY

▶ Page 13: **Bubble Quiz**

A. You can dive when you're ten.

▶ Pages 14–15: **"Sea" What I Mean?**

1) H   2) C   3) G   4) B   5) I   6) A

7) J   8) E   9) D   10) K   11) L   12) F

The diver is saying she's low on air!

▶ Page 19: **Take Only Pictures, Leave Only Bubbles**

1) **C.** As tempting as it may be, don't try to hitchhike on animals. It's extremely stressful for them.

2) **A.** Picking up plants and animals can hurt or even kill them. Collecting other objects can disturb the environment for other people, too. When underwater, take nothing but pictures!

3) **B.** To avoid harm to you and the animals, don't feed marine life unless you're with an expert who says it's okay and shows you how. Same goes for touching and handling sea creatures.

4) **C.** Never touch corals, and definitely don't stand on them. Even just a little contact can hurt them.

▶ Page 36: **Say It Like a Submariner!**

1) C   2) G   3) A   4) F   5) E

6) I   7) D   8) J   9) H   10) B

"Dancing with the fat lady" refers to the large size of the periscope. You have to hold both handles to swivel it around.